Beadle and Company

Beadle's dime Union song book no. 2 : comprising new and popular patriotic songs for the times

Beadle and Company

Beadle's dime Union song book no. 2 : comprising new and popular patriotic songs for the times

ISBN/EAN: 9783337306472

Printed in Europe, USA, Canada, Australia, Japan

Cover: Foto ©Thomas Meinert / pixelio.de

More available books at **www.hansebooks.com**

BEADLE'S

DIME

UNITED STATES OF AMERICA · ONE DIME

UNION SONG BOOK

No. 2.

COMPRISING NEW AND POPULAR

PATRIOTIC SONGS

FOR THE TIMES.

NEW YORK AND LONDON:
Beadle and Company, 141 William St., N Y.
44 PATERNOSTER ROW, LONDON.

CONTENTS.

iv   CONTENTS.

BEADLE'S
DIME UNION SONG BOOK
No. 2.

The Star-Flag.

Air—*The Star-Spangled Banner.*

When our fathers in vain sought redress from the throne,
  And the tyrant grew mad in his thirst for dominion,
Earth shook while the bugle of conflict was blown;
  And our eagle unfolded his newly-fledged pinion.
      Men with hair thin and white,
     . Bared their arms for the fight,
And the lad of sixteen made the dull weapon bright;
  While gilding the battle-storm, rolling in wrath,
  The star-flag of Freedom streamed full on their path.

The bird to that banner forever allied,
  Was born in the cloud, and baptized by the thunder;
And deeply in blood will his talons be dyed,
  Ere its clustering stars shall be riven asunder.
      And fiercely their light,
     Through the smoke of the fight,
Shall flash, making traitors grow pale at the sight;
  And the sun, overtaken by death, shall grow cold,
  When the banner we hail is no longer unrolled.

Black treason shall never put foot on the flag ;
 That floated the blast when Cornwallis was taken;
And ere it give place to a Palmetto rag,
 The dead on the fields of their fame will awaken,
   Oh, shall it be furled,
   Bringing night on the world,
While the house of our fathers in ruin is hurled !
 The brigand and traitor may hear a reply
 In the clash of our steel and the rallying cry.

Our bold Harry Clay loved this land of the free—
 His name from old Jackson we will not dissever;
Then spliced be your Ash to the Hickory-tree,
 And let them be symbols of Union forever.
   Without fear in their hearts,
   Well they acted their parts,
Though traitors showered on them their deadliest darts;
 And true to their Maker, and faithful to man,
 The standard of Freedom they bore in the van.

From the North to the Tropic shall float on the gale
 Our star-flag, upheld by the brave and the just;
Though a wretched Disunion banditti assail,
 They shall not drag down its proud eagle to dust.
   Then arm for the strife,
   Give them war to the knife,
And light in the balance with Union hold life ;
 Our flag to the breeze that a Washington blest,
 Though torn must wave over Charleston again.

Union Forever.

Copied by permission of FIRTH, POND & Co., Music Publishers,
547 Broadway, N. Y., owners of the copyright.

The Union of States forever will stand,
    The watchword of Freedom and Fame,
A refuge for all from tyranny's sway,
    An altar for Liberty's flame.
That Banner, bedecked by Heaven's own tints,
    When threatened with insult or scorn,
Each Patriot heart will rally around,
    To shelter its folds from the storm!

CHORUS.

The Union of States forever will stand,
    Defying oppression's dark blight;
Forever our flag will wave o'er the land,
    The ensign of Freedom and Light.

Columbia's sons triumphant will breast
    Disunion's tempestuous sea,
Our grand old Ship forever will sail,
    The pride of the brave and the free.
What God in his mercy hath wisely ordained,
    Forever a nation to stand,
Not all foreign factions or traitors combined
    Can ever defame or disband

CHORUS.

The Union of States forever will stand,
    Defying oppression's dark blight;
Forever our Flag will wave o'er the land,
    The ensign of Freedom and Light.

Where Liberty dwells, there is my Country.

Copied by permission of HORACE WATERS, Music Publisher, 481 Broadway, N. Y., owner of the copyright.

Where Liberty dwells is my country;
There, only there; there, only there;
Where Liberty dwells is my country;
There, and only there.*
Though storms should howl around her,
And skies be overcast,
And the good ship seem just to founder,
Still, boys, we give to the blast:
Chorus.—Where Liberty dwells, etc.

That land, we will defend her,
While floats our flag on high;
Our motto is, " Never surrender,"
Fight till we conquer or die. [Chorus.

That star-sprent flag once covered
Our Washington, the blest;
That eagle victorious has hovered
Long o'er our bravest and best. [Chorus.

And know, there's One who never
Bids a good cause go down;
God reigns, and His favor is ever
With us—with our foes, His frown. [Chorus.

Sing, then; bid those who love us,
Join in our song so free;
The heavens are smiling above us,
Success, peace and liberty. [Chorus.

* Repeat first four lines at commencement of each stanza.

Summons to the North.

AIR—*To the West—to the West.*

To the field! to the field! where our comrades now
    stand,
For the cause of the Union, the life of our land!
Where the sons of the North for their liberties fight,
And the men of all nations combine for the right;
Where the children of Erin with Britons conjoin,
And the Gaul and the German press loin unto loin;
And the men of Italia and Hungary true
Are surrounding the Flag of the Red, White and Blue!

CHORUS.

To the field! to the field! let no freeman delay!
For our cause is the Union's, our time is to-day!
If the power of the Northland triumphant would be,
It must rise like the tempest, and surge like the sea.

'Tis a cause—'tis a cause that makes heroes of all;
For the Union, the Union to conquer or fall!
'Tis the cause of mankind, 'tis the cause of the world,
That our swords are unsheathed for, our banners
    unfurled!
And the heart of the vassal on Muscovite plains,
And the soul of the Polander, weary of chains,
And the pulse of the Magyar, the brain of the Greek,
Will respond with the hopes that their lips dare not
    speak.
        To the field! etc.

The Flag and the Union.

Air—*Bay of Biscay, O!*

Loud roared Disunion's thunder,
 And Treason's fires burned red;
Our nation, rent asunder,
 Beheld the tempest dread;
  From Sumter's blazing spars,
  Our glorious flag of stars,
   Torn away,
   Prostrate lay,
  Under sway of Rebels, O!

But upward rose our Nation,
 Aroused by war's alarms;
With one loud declaration
 The people sprung to arms—
  "Our Flag," they cried, "shall wave!
  Our Union we will save!
   Clear the way,
   For the fray!
  We'll repay these Rebels, O!"

"Our course by heaven is guided—
 Its goal yet shines afar—
Our Union undivided—
 Our flag with every star!
  From Rio Grande's shore,
  To ice-bound Labrador,
   Land and sea
   Shall be free
  From the sway of Rebels, O!"

Draw the Sword, Northland.

AIR—*Draw the Sword, Scotland.*

Draw the sword, Northland! Northland! Northland!
  Too long have we parleyed with insolent foes;
Arise for the Union, Union, Union!
  Even as for freedom our fathers arose!
From valleys and mountains, clustering, clustering,
  From forest and prairie, and shores of the sea;
For Freedom's great battle-field mustering, mustering,
  Beneath the star-banner, the Flag of the Free!
Draw the sword, Northland! Northland! Northland!
  Charge on Rebellion and all its dark powers;
Strike for the Union, Union, Union!
  He who holds back is no comrade of ours!

Sheathe the sword, Northland! Northland! North-
    land!
  Only when Rebels no longer contend—
Only when Union, Union, Union!
  Shall weld a new bond that no Treason can rend!
When the dread struggle is over, over,
  And Liberty's duty is fairly done,
We will offer our hands to the vanquished, van-
    quished,
  And bid them be once more the Many in One!
Sheathe the sword, Northland! Northland! North-
    land!
  Only when Treason no longer lowers!
Only when Union, Union, Union!
  For all the great Future, is ours, still ours!

The Great Union Club.

BY ROBERT M. HART.

AIR—*Villikins and Dinah*.

There is an old gent and his name it is Abe,
He is a rail-splitter, for so it is said,
But for the whole Union he ever was true,
And thought it a farce to *split it in two*.

CHORUS.

Rub-be-dub, rub-be-dub, rub-be-dub, dub,
Oh march to the tap of the rub-be-dub, dub,
Old Abe he is raising a " Great Union *Club*,"
To give the Seceshers a very hard rub.

When Abe was elected 'twas late in the Fall,
As President, over Seceshers and all,
And by all the rails in the Union did swear—
Jacksonian like—to act on the square.

Seceshers were trying to frighten old Abe,
By blowing and stealing—their favorite trade—
But when they had made a considerable noise,
Old Abe gave a yell for some of " The Boys."

The yell it was heard, and it had its effect,
To play " Help your neighbor," " The Boys " did
          " collect ;
Secesh " couldn't see it"—he found he was matched,
Had counted his chickens before they were hatched.

To fence in the Union, without any *bars*,
Old Abe is at work by the light of the *Stars ;*
It soon will be finished, and when he is through,
He'll paint it all over with Red, White and Blue.

Hurrah for the Land we Love.

Air—*A Life on the Ocean Wave.*

Hurrah for the land we love!
Hurrah for the laws we keep!
Our Banner we've nailed above,
And our Faith is anchored deep!
Let the trembling knave betray,
Let the paltry changeling fly;
There will come an answering day,
For our Cause can never die.

CHORUS.

Then, hurrah for the land we love,
And hurrah for the laws we keep!
Our Banner is nailed above,
And our Faith is anchored deep!

A lesson the traitors teach,
And a lesson the cowards give,
'Tis easy the Right to preach,
But 'tis harder the Right to live!
We laugh at the weak-kneed crew
Who shiver on Faction's shore;
But with Brothers yet firm and true,
We'll meet Disunion's roar.
Then hurrah, etc

The Flag of the Free.

AIR—*O saw ye the Lass with the bonny blue E'en?*

Oh saw ye the Flag with the Thirty-four Stars?
'Tis red with the glories of Liberty's wars ;
'Tis bright as the sunbeam, and blue as the sky,
'Tis the loveliest banner that waveth on high.
The home of that Flag is each patriot's heart—
From Freedom and Union it never can part ;
For wherever it floateth, on land or on sea,
Every nation proclaims it the Flag of the Free !

Though the hand of dark Treason its luster would mar,
It shall yield not a stripe, it shall lose not a star ;
But forevermore planted on Liberty's rock,
Every storm it will breast, and defy every shock.
While the broad Mississippi flows down to the main,
And the blue Alleghanies arise from the plain—
While Niagara's waters unshackled shall be,
It will wave o'er our Union, the Flag of the Free !

Gathering Song.

Air—*Bonny Boat.*

Oh, gayly sound the bugles shrill,
Adown the mountain-glen,
And loudly on the breezes thrill
The songs of loyal men!
Still marching on with iron tramp
To battle's wild accords,
They point to vile Rebellion's camp,
And clash their fathers' swords!

Oh, proudly throbs each patriot's heart,
When, thundering from afar,
O'er woodland-glen, or mountain-crest,
Upswells the loud hurrah!
While trumpet-peal and rattling drum,
And wild artillery's roar,
Proclaim that Freedom's soldiers come
As came their sires of yore.

Liberty.

Air—*Somebody's Waiting for Somebody.*

Cloudy and dark is the heaven,
   Darksome and doubtful for Liberty;
But there's a cloud or two riven,
   Showing the bright light of Liberty;
Out of the midst of all gloom,
   Shines the fair promise of Liberty—
Over each patriot's tomb,
   Rises the day-star of Liberty,
   Rises the day-star of Liberty!

There will be battles to fight,
   Battles defending our Liberty!
There will be traitors to smite,
   Traitors who strike at our Liberty!
But when our triumph shall come,
   Over the foemen of Liberty,
Who will consider the sum
   Spent in defense of our Liberty?
   Spent in defense of our Liberty?

Lift up the Banner of Stars,
   Fling out the colors of Liberty;
Over all shackles and bars,
   We will march forward to Liberty!
Union and laws we'll defend,
   Guided and guarded by Liberty,
Till, at the glorious end,
   All the world shares in our Liberty,
   All the world shares in our Liberty!

Wife of my Bosom.

Air—*Kathleen Mavourneen.*

Wife of my bosom, the midnight hangs o'er me,
    And shadow and silence encompass our camp;
Oh, dark is my heart, like the darkness before me,
    Wife of my bosom, while lonely I tramp;
'Tis not that I falter, or fear the red morrow,
    When true men give battle to rebels forsworn,
But the heart of each soldier may have its own sorrow,
    And 'tis thinking of thee, love, makes mine so forlorn.

Wife of my bosom, the night-hours are lonely,
    And lonesome my heart, as I tread my dark round;
But through all the dim watches I've thought of thee
    only,
Wife of my bosom, with yearning profound.
Now the day breaks, and the drums call to battle,
    While cannon's deep thunder announces the morn;
Full gladly I welcome the din and the rattle,
    'Tis only for thee, wife, my heart is forlorn.

Wife of my bosom, in God's blessed keeping
    Our lives are still mingled, though parted are we;
Above us He watcheth, with mercies unsleeping,
    Wife of my bosom, o'er thee and o'er me.
I dare the wild conflict, where lives must be rended,
    But faith in my bosom now brightens with morn;
By thy prayers in the past I have still been defended,
    And He whom we trust will not leave thee forlorn.

The Union Sacrifice.

BY MRS. METTA V. VICTOR.

"Who will save the land we cherish?
People! what have you to give,
That our country may not perish—
That our liberties may live?"

Hark! the answer quickly thrilling:—
"*Half a million volunteers*
Rally round our standard, filling
Freedom's air with freemen's cheers!

"See our men go forth to battle,
Take the soldier's hardy fare,
Face the fearful cannon's rattle,
Danger, death and drudgery bear.

"What give you, heroic women,
Loving mothers, tender wives?"
Comes the answer superhuman:
"*We give up our dear ones' lives!*

"We remain at home to suffer—
Not to rest in idle ease.
Men's stern duties may be rougher,
But they can not equal these;—

" Nights of wretched, restless tossing,
   Guessing at the toils unshared—
Fields and streams at midnight crossing,
   Keeping lonely picket guard;

" Days of terror and of weeping—
   Of suspense that holds the breath,
While the rosy infant, sleeping,
   Dreams not of its father's death.

" News that comes too sure and often
   To the mothers at their work,—
With no circumstance to soften
   All the woes that in it lurk—

" How the sons, at home surrounded
   By their fond and patient care,
On the battle-field lie wounded,
   Dying, dead,—no mother there !"

Rich men give up golden treasures—
   Money, ships and merchandise;
Brave men give up care and pleasures
   For the liberties they prize !

But no holier gifts are proffered
   By the hero's heart and hand,
Than the sacrifices offered
   By the *women* of the Land !

Blue Jackets, Fall in!

AIR—*Bonny Dundee*.

Let the plotters of treason their standard forsake,
And abandon the eagle for vulture or snake;
But the man who's a true man, wherever he be,
Follows only one banner—the Flag of the Free.

CHORUS.

Then sound to the color! Blue Jackets, fall in!
There's a march to be made, and a battle to win!
There are rebels and traitors to scour from the lea,
So make room for our banner—the Flag of the Free.

To the soft southern breezes our colors are spread,
By the bravest and noblest they're followed and led,
And wherever they wave, in the battle's red van,
They are symbols of justice and freedom for man.
　　　　Then sound to the color, etc.

Jeff. Davis may menace, and Beauregard rage,
And defyingly strut their brief hour on the stage;
But their empire is ruin—their triumph is shame,
And the wrath they provoke will consume them like
　　　flame.
　　　　Then sound to the color, etc.

Song of the Zouaves.

Air—*The Plains of Mexico.*

Dash on, dash on, my gallant Zouaves,
   Where dangers darkly frown ;
Let Freedom bravely nerve your arms,
   Strike every traitor down.
What though their murd'rous squadrons stand,
   In stern and fierce array ;
We'll make them feel our sweeping charge,
   And quickly clear the way.

This Union, which so long hath been
   The shelt'ring home of all
Fair Freedom's valiant, holy band,
   Shall not by traitors fall ;
But it will stand, through storm and strife,
   The home of Freedom's band,
And naught shall cause its overthrow,
   While strength lies in our hand.

Though years may roll their onward course,
   Our hands shall ne'er be stayed;
Till Freedom's land be free from strife,
   And in sweet peace arrayed.
And now, farewell to home and friends,
   And if we ne'er return,
'Twill be because the gallant Sixth
   All death and danger spurn.

The Northmen are Coming.

AIR—*I'm Going to be Married.*

The Northmen are coming, Oho! oho!
The Northmen are coming, Oho! oho!
 The Northmen, the Northmen,
 The warriors of Freedom!
The Northmen are coming, Oho! oho!

Their star-spangled banners I see, I see!
The plume-crested horsemen I see, I see!
 Down mountain and valley the hosts are streaming,
And shouting the battle-cry, "One and Free."
  The Northmen are coming, etc.

The peal of their bugles I hear, I hear!
The clangor of trumpets I hear, I hear!
 The banners outflame like the blazing morn,
O'er billows of bayonet, sword and spear.
  The Northmen are coming, etc.

With rattle of musket they come, they come!
With thunder of cannon, they come, they come!
 With tempest of fire, and storm of steel,
To drive out the traitors from Freedom's home.
  The Northmen are coming, etc.

The boom of their cannon is Tyranny's knell;
Wherever they battle shall Liberty dwell;
 They fight for the holiest hope of man,
They triumph with Washington, Bruce and Tell
  The Northmen are coming, etc.

They come with the banners our sires unfurled,
Unfurled for the exile, the bondman, the world,
 And Heaven shall speed their victorious march,
Till Liberty's foes to the dust be hurled.
  The Northmen are coming, etc.

The Volunteer Yankee Doodle of '61.

Yankee Doodle comes to town,
  Walking on his feet, sir!
Shouldered gun and soldier's gown,
  Yankee can't be beat, sir!
In his bosom burns a love
  For his glorious country,
Sparkling like the stars above,
  Ay! much less it won't be.
Yankee Doodle, keep it up;
  Yankee doodle dandy,
Plant your bayonet on the top,
  And wi' the gun be handy!
       Yankee Doodle, etc.

Yankee Doodle marches on
  Till the foes he'll meet, sir!
Shoots at least a dozen down—
  Yankee can't be beat, sir!
For the Stars and Stripes he'll fight,
  For the Constitution;
Put the enemy to flight,
  End the Revolution.
Yankee Doodle, keep it up;
  Yankee doodle dandy,
Plant your bayonet on the top,
  And wi' the gun be handy!

Victory gained, he takes his ease
  At his country seat, sir!
Following the arts of peace,
  Yankee can't be beat, sir!
Plenty yields his native soil,
  Faithful to his labor;
And the Lord rewards his toil,
  Grants him every favor.
Yankee Doodle, keep it up;
  Yankee doodle dandy,
Plant your corn, and reap your crop,
  And wi' the plough be handy!

Flag Song.

Air—The Land of the Leal.

Come, lift it on high, boys!
Once more let it fly, boys,
We'll fight and we'll die
  For the Red, White and Blue!
'Twas hallowed before, boys,
In battles of yore, boys,
We'll guard it once more
  With our bosoms so true!

Then fling out the flag, boys,
From spar and from crag, boys,
No freeman shall lag
  While there's fighting to do:
To the front of the fray, boys,
We'll soon find the way, boys,
And yet win the day
  For our Red, White and Blue!

Our Country, Now and Ever.

Copied by permission of HORACE WATERS, Music Publisher,
481 Broadway, N. Y., owner of the copyright.

Our Country, now and ever!
 Land of the good and free!
What daring hand would sever
 The ties of Liberty?
Let him be known as traitor,
 And traitor shall he be;
Who would insult this nation
 Must first himself be free.

For such are slaves and cowards—
 Their names a thing of shame;
To endless time our Union
 Will but increase in fame.
Fight, comrades, for our nation,
 For Freedom's holy light;
In union is salvation,
 God will protect the right.

My Love he is a Zou-zu.

My love is a Zou-zu so gallant and bold;
He's rough and he's handsome, scarce nineteen years
   old,
To show off in Washington, he has left his own dear,
And my heart is a-breaking because he's not here.

CHORUS.

For his spirit was brave; it was fierce to behold,
In a young man bred a Zou-zu, only nineteen years old.

His parents taught him to be a Cavalier,
But the life of a Zou-zu he much did prefer ;
For his heart's with his Country in right or in wrong,
And in Richmond with Burnside, he'll be afore long.
For his spirit, etc.

My fond heart is beating for him constantly,
But I fear his affections may waver from me ;
For a sweetheart can be found in each State, I am
   told, .
By a young man, a Zou-zu, only nineteen years old.
For his spirit, etc.

And now for my Zou-zu I grieve and repine,
For fear that his brave heart may never be mine ;
All the wealth of Jeff. Davis in cotton or gold,
I would give for my Zou-zu, only nineteen years old.
For his spirit, etc.

The Stripes and Stars.

Air—*The Low-backed Car.*

Let cowards shirk their duty,
    And falter from the fray;
My post I'll find, nor shrink behind,
    When honor calls away.
For Union and for Freedom,
    I'll wield a sword or gun,
And take my stand, for laws and land,
    Till the battle's nobly won.

CHORUS.

For I follow the Stripes and Stars,
No matter for wounds or scars,
    And I'll act my part,
    With my arm and heart,
In defense of the Stripes and Stars.

The truth is past denying,
    That danger's close at hand,
And I do love, all things above,
    My own dear native land.
So where the conflict rages,
    And where our foemen be,
To stand or fall, at Union's call,
    There is the place for me.   [*Chorus.*

May God bless those who love me,
    And those I love defend;
If life I give, to those who live
    My dear ones I commend.
But while the cannon's booming,
    And trumpets loudly blare,
The Union's cause, the land and laws,
    Must be my only care.   [*Chorus.*

Hark to the Tread.

Hark ! hark ! to the tread
  Of men of olden time,
The footsteps of the mighty dead
  Still sounding on sublime.
Our Union's strong foundations
  They planted broad and deep,
And we, among the nations,
  Our own proud place will keep !

CHORUS.

  Join hearts ! join hands !
  A wreath of glory twine,
  Of palm and mountain pine.
    Strike hands !
    The Union stands !

Now, now is the hour
  To let foul Treason know,
That patriot legions have the power
  To work its overthrow ;
That while the conflict rages,
  And hearts are sorely tried,
The HAND that guides the ages
  Is lifted on our side.

Tell, tell to your sons
  The story of your sires,
And that the pledge forever runs
  To guard their sacred fires.
Tell them the great AVENGER
  Unsheathed his awful sword,
When FREEDOM was in danger,
  And smote the rebel horde !

The Old Flag Alone.

Air—*Old Folks at Home.*

Strongly the traitors now are banded,
    Fierce are they grown,
By rebel demagogues commanded,
    Laws overthrown ;
Cursing the banner of their fathers,
    Madly they swarm,
Hurling against the Rock of Union,
    Daring Rebellion's storm.
        But true hearts can never falter,
            Now their faith is shown ;
        So we stand by Freedom's altar,
            True to the Old Flag alone !

Once in the land we all were true men,
    Joined hand in hand ;
Now Treason's madness makes them foemen,
    Cumbering the land ;
So we must treat them as we find them,
    "Enemies in war ;"
Fighting against the Flag of Union,
    Friends they can never be, more,
        Our true hearts shall never falter,
            Here our faith is shown,
        Standing now by Freedom's altar,
            True to the Old Flag alone !

The Birth of Our Banner.

BY ROBERT M. HART.

AIR—*Columbia, the Gem of the Ocean.*

When the dawn of creation was budding,
   To blossom in bright, balmy day,
The Goddess of Light, at her waking,
   Was shrouded with curtains of spray,
That rose as the incense of morning,
   From valleys resplendent with dew,
To deck the broad ocean of distance
   In tints of the White, Red and Blue.

And far in the blue dome of heaven,
   Were stars with a soft, holy ray,
That have shone in an unbroken union
   While ages have mouldered away;
And Freedom, when journeying hither,
   The earth with its blessings to strew,
Has gathered these trophies of glory,
   As gems for the White, Red and Blue.

When man braved the wrath of Jehovah,
   The flood-gates of heaven arose
To deluge the earth, in his anger,
   And drive from existence his foes;
Still justice was tempered with mercy—
   On cloud-crested banners he drew
His promise to all generations,
   In symbols of White, Red and Blue.

And thus is our Banner of Freedom
   But tints of the glories above
Of Him who has made us a nation,
   And bound us with garlands of love—
Which none on the earth can dissever,
   For each on our altars renew
Our oath of unshaken devotion
   And trust in the White, Red and Blue.

"E Pluribus Unum."

BY JOHN PIERPONT.

AIR—*Star-Spangled Banner.*

The harp of the minstrel with melody rings
  When the Muses have taught him to touch and to
    tune it;
But though it may have a full octave of strings,
  To both maker and minstrel the harp is a unit.
So the power that creates our republic of States,
  Into harmony brings them at different dates;
    And the thirteen or thirty, the Union once done,
    Are "*E Pluribus Unum*"—of many made one.

The science that weighs in her balance the spheres,
  And watched them since first the Chaldean began it,
Now and then, as she counts them and measures their
    years,
  Brings into our system and names a new planet.
Yet the old and new stars—Venus, Neptune and Mars,
As they drive round the sun their invisible cars,
  Whether faster or slower their races they run,
  Are "*E Pluribus Unum*"—of many made one.

Of that system of spheres, should but one fly the track,
  Or with others conspire for a general dispersion,
By the great central orb they would all be brought back,
  And held, each in her place, by a wholesome coercion.
Should one daughter of light be indulged in her flight,
They would all be engulfed by old Chaos and Night;
  So must none of our sisters be suffered to run,
  For, "*E Pluribus Unum*"—we all go if one.

Let the demon of discord our melody mar,
  Or Treason's red hand rend our Union asunder,
Break one string from our harp, or extinguish one star,
  The whole system's ablaze with its lightning and
    thunder.
Let the discord be hushed! Let the traitors be crushed!
Though "Legion" their name, all with victory flushed!
  For aye must our motto stand, fronting the sun:
  "*E Pluribus Unum*"—*Though many, we're* ONE.

The Northern Hurrah.

AIR—*Sprig of Shillaly.*

Oh, brave is the soul of a true Union man!
He arms for the battle—he springs to the van,
  To the war-shout of freemen—the Northern Hurrah!
His heart bears no malice—his lips have no lie!
For the old Constitution his pulses beat high;
And in camp or in action, in march or at rest,
'Tis the love of our Union that leaps from his breast
  In the war-shout of freemen—the Northern Hurrah!
    Hurrah! hurrah! hurrah!

Oh, the slogan of Scotland is startling and shrill,
And the loud Marseillaise every Frenchman will thrill;
  But there's never a shout like the Northern Hurrah!
Let the Turkman cry "Allah!" while charging his foe—
And the Briton, "St. George!" with each resolute blow;
But the wildest of war-cries, the slogan most grand,
Is the chorus that leaps from the heart of our land
  In the war-shout of freedom—the Northern Hurrah!
    Hurrah! hurrah! hurrah!

From the mountains of Hampshire, the headlands of Maine,
Alleghany's blue peaks and Nevada's high chain,
Rolleth down, like the thunder, this Northern Hurrah;
And the rocks and the vales, and the waters profound,
And the forests and prairies re-echo the sound;
And the voice of great cities, from east and from west,
Swells the shout of the free for the land they love best,
  In a war-hymn for freedom—the Northern Hurrah!
    Hurrah! hurrah! hurrah!

The Harp of Old Erin and banner of Stars.

AIR—*St. Patrick's Day.*

The war-trump has sounded, our rights are in danger ;
  Shall the brave sons of Erin be deaf to the call,
When freedom demands of both native and stranger,
  Their aid, lest the greatest of nations should fall ?
Shall this banner, so dear to the exiles of Gael,
  By traitors and rebels, in anarchy's school,
Be trailed in the dust, disgraced in the vale,
  While our people, the sov'reign, in equity rule ?

No : I swear by the love that we bear our old Sire-land,
  And the vows we have pledged to this home of the free,
As we'd sheathe our swords in the foes of dear Ireland,
  We will use them as freely 'gainst traitors to thee.
Need we fear for our cause when true hearts uphold it ?
  See the men of all nations now march to the wars ;
And shall Erin's stout hearts stand by and behold it,
  Nor strike in their might for the Banner of Stars?

No, no ; with their life's blood they'll guard the rich treasure ;
  See how they respond to the call, "Shoulder Arms !"
Though endeared by those sacred ties, love beyond measure
  Of bosom-friends, children, and beauty's sweet charms,
Yet they leave all behind, and equip for the battle
  Between freedom and rapine, like true sons of Mars ;
They'll conquer though traitors their cannon may rattle,
  And bring back triumphant the Banner of Stars.

Oh ! long may our flags wave in Union together,
  And the harp of green Erin still kiss the same breeze,
And brave ev'ry storm that beclouds the fair weather,
  Till our harp, like the Stars, floats o'er rivers and seas.
God prosper manly soul-heart, on both land and ocean,
  That goes in defiance of danger and scars,
And send them safe home, to their wives and their sweet-
    hearts,
  With the harp of old Erin and Banner of Stars.

The Delaware Volunteers.

Come all you young men that do intend to roam
From the State of Delaware, a long way from home,
Cruising down around the banks of the Southern
　　　States hi O,
Through sweet and shady groves,
Through the rebel States we'll ramble and we'll hang
　　Jeff. Davis, O.

There's fishes in the Delaware that's fitting for our use,
Likewise the sugar-cane that yields to us its'juice,
There's plenty of good Union men for the Stars and
　　Stripes, you know,
　　　　Cruising down around the banks, etc.

Come all you young girls, and spin us some yarn,
You can make us clothing to keep ourselves warm,
And you can knit and spin, my girls, while we can
　　reap and mow ;
　　　　.Cruising down around, etc.

If any of them Southerners dare to come nigh,
We'll rush into the States, and conquer or we'll die ;
We'll rush into the ranks and strike a powerful blow,
　　　　Cruising down around, etc.

Our Flag.

BY R. W. MACGOWAN.

AIR—*The American Boy.*

We'll rally round the same old Flag
  Our fathers did of yore,
And bravely fight beneath those folds
  They hallowed with their gore ;
We'll guard it as a sacred trust
  With our devoted band,
And shield it from the treachery
  Of the Southron's murd'rous hand.

What though we had a traitor Twiggs,
  An Arnold we'd before ;
But we have still our loyal North,
  That keeps the oath it swore.
As brave as ever to the breeze
  Our noble Flag's unfurled,
The pride and blessing of our land,
  The envy of the world.

And eager thousands grasp the sword,
  The scabbard thrown away ;
With willing hands and faithful hearts,
  They're ready for the fray,
To teach the Southern fratricide
  The Stars and Stripes shall wave
O'er this the land of liberty,
  The birthplace of the brave.

RESPECTFULLY DEDICATED TO THE 69TH REG'T., N. Y. S. M.

Sweet Maid of Erin.

BY ROBERT M. HART.

AIR—*Kathleen Mavourneen.*

Sweet Maid of Erin, the war-cry is sounding,
  The bugle's loud pealing is heard o'er the plain,
While Death on his charger in battle is bounding,
  And leaving behind him our patriot slain.
Thou hast not forgotten the friends that you parted,
  To battle for country, for God, and our right;
And sad are thy tears for the lone broken-hearted,
  Who silently languish in grief's fearful night;
Sweet Maid of Erin, they welcome thy footsteps,
  And pray for thee daily and Erin go Bragh.

Sweet Maid of Erin, the green grass is springing
  Beside where the loved ones of Erin lie low,
And down in the village the church-bells are ringing—
  Alas! how thy minstrel is cast down with woe.
He has not forgotten thy love and affection—
  The last parting kiss and thy musical sigh—
They linger together in fond recollection,
  And cheer him to duty when dangers are nigh.
Sweet Maid of Erin, the song of thy minstrel
  Is, God bless Columbia and Erin go Bragh.

Sweet Maid of Erin, the Shamrock and Thistle
  Are linked with the Star-crested Banner to-day,
And, waving in glory where fierce weapons bristle,
  Are emblems of greatness in Freedom's affray.
We have not forgotten the fond hope of freemen,
  The home in the West for the true and the brave;
And Celts ne'er will yield, for the daring shall lead them
  To triumph o'er Treason, or sink in the grave.
Sweet Maid of Erin, though far in the distance,
  I still love my darling, and Erin go Bragh.

Stand by the Union.

AIR—*Wait for the Wagon.*

Fellow-citizens and soldiers! I've a word or two to say,
There's no use to dodge the question, or to flout the facts
    away;
If a man is not a traitor, he'll not fear to show his hand,
And unless we all are rebels, we must by the Union stand.

CHORUS.
Stand by the Union! Stand by the Union!
Stand by the Union! and be on the right side.

When soldiers' plumes are dyed with blood, the good old
    hearty red,
We'd better mark the knave who wears white feathers on
    his head;
While batteries menace Washington, and rebel armies rise,
A coward or a traitor's he who prates of " Compromise."
        Stand by the Union, etc.

The only Compromise we'll make is at the cannon's mouth,
The only terms of Peace we'll give—Submission by the
    South:
One only power must rule the land—it can't be ruled by
    two—
And we must prove who strongest are—the Traitors or the
    True!
        Stand by the Union, etc.

'Tis ours to meet and measure now the powers of Right
    and Wrong,
While they are weak with Slavery, in Union we are strong;
For all that Washington bequeathed to humankind we
    fight—
Hurrah, then, for the Union! and may God protect the
    Right!
        Stand by the Union, etc.

Drummer Boy of the National Greys.

See the gallant Drummer Boy,
How his face lights up with joy,
As he takes his envied place
In the corps of the National Greys.
    Noble Clarie, Patriot Clarie!
Drummer of the National Greys.

All the children in the street
Strive with Clarie to compete,
As upon his drum he plays
In the corps of the National Greys.
    Noble Clarie, Warrior Clarie!
Drummer of the National Greys.

Ah! but Clarie 'll have to go
Where his own life-blood may flow,—
This he knows, yet firmly stays
In the corps of the National Greys.
    Noble Clarie, Faithful Clarie!
Drummer of the National Greys.

Tho' the direst ills betide,
Clarie's heart beats high with pride
When he hears the shouts of praise
Echoing for the National Greys.
    Noble Clarie, Hero Clarie!
Drummer of the National Greys.

Clarie's bosom knew no fear,
Tho' his eye betray'd a tear
When his Mother's sadden'd gaze
Rested on the National Greys.
    Noble Clarie, Loving Clarie!
Drummer of the National Greys.

"Never shall the traitor drag
From its height our Country's Flag!"
Thus, he loyalty displays
In the corps of the National Greys.
    Noble Clarie, Brave young Clarie!
Drummer of the National Greys.

Trusting in the God of love,
Clarie looks with faith above,
Pray'r and meekness guide his ways
In the corps of the National Greys.
　　Noble Clarie, Christian Clarie!
Drummer of the National Greys.

Hark! that musket's direful sound!
See the fatal ball rebound!
Suddenly a piercing cry
Rends the air and cleaves the sky;
　　'Tis from Clarie, Martyr Clarie!
Loved of all the National Greys.　-

Tears, those Soldiers' eyes suffuse;
Sad and solemn is the news;
Clarie rudely from them torn,—
From their ranks forever gone.
　　Mirthful Clarie, Buoyant Clarie!
Fav'rite with the National Greys.

Clarie now lies still and cold
(Only twelve brief summers old)
Low beneath the mould'ring sod,
But his soul has gone to God.
　　Gentle Clarie, Youthful Clarie!
Mourn'd of all the National Greys.

Muffled is the rolling drum,
Hush'd the busy children's hum,
Agonized a father's brow,—
All in deep submission bow.
　　Spirit Clarie, Blessed Clarie!
Gather'd with the angels now.

Sadden'd is the humble home,
There no more his step will come,
But his songs of praise will rise
In a home beyond the skies.
　　Happy Clarie, Ransom'd Clarie!
Seraph bright in Paradise.

Following the Drum.

Air—*Over the Mountain.*

Up from the valley deeps,
　Down from the crags,
Out from the forest-aisles,
　Waving our flags—
Marching with warlike tread,
　Forward we come,
Sons of America,
　Following the drum !
　　　Shouting our battle-cries,
　　　　Forward we come,
　　　Sons of America,
　　　　Following the drum !

Down from New England hills,
　Out from New York,
Over the Jersey plains,
　Strong for our work—
From Pennsylvania's glens,
　From Indiana,
Up from the O-hi-o,
　Under our banner.

Michigan's riflemen,
　Oregon's scouts,
Landsmen and mariners,
　Mingling their shouts ;
Under the Flag of Stars—
　Waving still high—
Still for the Union, boys,
　Stand we or die !

Victory's Band.

AIR—*Dixie's Land.*

We're marching under the Flag of Union,
Keeping step in brave communion!
March away! march away! away! Victory's band
Right down upon the ranks of rebels,
Tramp them underfoot like pebbles,
March away! march away! away! Victory's band

CHORUS.

Oh! we're marching on to Victory!
    Hurrah! hurrah!
In Victory's band we'll sweep the land,
 And fight or die for Victory!
    Away! away!
We'll fight or die for Victory!

The rebels want a mongrel nation,
Union and Confederation!
March away! march away! away! Victory's band!
But we don't trust in things two-sided,
And go for Union undivided,
March away! march away! away! Victory's band!
   Oh! we're marching, etc.

We're marching down on Dixie's regions,
With Freedom's flag and Freedom's legions,
March away! march away! away! Victory's band!
We're rolling down, a "Pending Crisis,"
With cannon-balls for Compromises,
March away! march away! away! Victory's band!
   Oh! we're marching, etc.

Mustering-Chorus.

Air—*The Merry Swiss Boy.*

Come arouse, men, arouse, men, the trumpet calls,
  Every patriot must off to the fray !   [*Repeat.*]
    The land we love is girt with foes,
    The flame of war still fiercer glows ;
Come, arouse, then, arouse, then, the trumpet calls,
  Every patriot must haste to the fray !

'Tis no time, men, no time, men, for fear or pause,
  While the trumpet is calling away !   [*Repeat.*]
    The Union's heart is rent in twain,
    'Tis ours to bind its cords again !
'Tis no time, men, no time, men, for fear or pause,
  While the trumpet is calling away !

Then, away, men, away, men, to follow our flag,
  Wheresoever it leads the way ;   [*Repeat.*]
    Let factions cease, let parties die,
    Let Union be our only cry—
And away, men, away, men, to follow our flag,
  Wheresoever it leads the way !

Begone, Sesesh!

AIR—*Begone, Dull Care.*

Begone, Sesesh! I bid thee begone from me!
Begone, Sesesh! you'd better make haste and flee!
    Long time you have been bullying here,
      And fain would Union kill;
    But, we all now swear,
      You never shall have your will!

Old Sesesh! I've known you in days gone by,
Old Sesesh! you wanted to *nul-li-fy!*
    Long time ago you badgered us,
      And tried, the land to rule,
    But we flogged you well with a *Hickory* rod,
      In brave old Jackson's school!

Begone, Sesesh! in South Carolina rest!
Begone, Sesesh! the snake is your proper crest!
    We've found out all your snakish ways,
      And drawn your serpent teeth,
    And wherever the foot of Freedom falls,
      Your head shall lie beneath!

The Patriot's Serenade.

BY ROBERT M. HART.

AIR—*Glory, Glory, Hallelujah.*

Look ye to our banner floating—
Freemen ever fondly doating—
Hirelings now so sadly gloating
At Treason's fearful sting.

CHORUS.

Glory, glory, be our anthem,
Glory, glory, be our anthem,
Praises to our Starry Banner,
As patriots, let us sing.

Hark! o'er hill and hamlet bounding,
Shouts of freemen now resounding,
All our enemies confounding—
Our eagle's on the wing.
Chorus.—Glory, glory, etc.

Spirits of the great departed!
Cheer the sad and broken-hearted—
Lead to victory those who started
To fight Rebellion's king.
Chorus.—Glory, glory, etc.

Rule, Columbia.

AIR—*Rule, Britannia.*

When tyrants fled our rescued land,
  And Freedom bless'd her sacred shrine,
Each patriot raised to heaven his hand,
  And swore to guard her rights divine.
      Rule, Columbia !
        The Union still must sway !
        Freemen rule America !

Our land is Freedom's chosen home,
  To all the world 'tis opened wide ;
To these fair shores let nations come,
  And all our bounteous soil divide.
      Rule, Columbia !
        The Union still must sway !
        Freemen rule America !

The Union is our children's dower,
  'Tis priceless as the air we breathe ;
While rebel arms defy its power,
  Our patriot swords we'll never sheathe !
      Rule, Columbia !
        The Union still must sway !
        Freemen rule America !

The Brave and Free.

Air—*The Pilot.*

Oh, comrades! 'tis a fearful strife
    That jars our land this day—
When brother strikes at brother's life,
    And sons their sires betray!
But He who rules each nation's right,
    Our sword and shield shall be!
Fear not! fear not! Jehovah's might
    Still guards the Brave and Free!

Though rebels swarm on every hand,
    And Treason spreads its snares,
Our Ship of State, by patriots mann'd,
    The Flag of Stars upbears!
Behind the clouds is sunshine bright,
    Whose beams we soon shall see!
Fear not! fear not! Jehovah's might
    Still guards the Brave and Free!

No craven doubt shall shake our trust
    In Union's righteous cause;
Our motives pure—our action just—
    For Freedom's Land, and Laws!
Against the foes of man we fight,
    And Victory ours shall be!
Fear not! fear not! Jehovah's might
    Still guards the Brave and Free!

Sweet is the Fight.

Air—Sparkling and Bright.

Sweet is the fight
For Freedom's right,
Though our heart's best blood be streaming;
By heroes led
Unto Glory's bed,
With lives our land redeeming!
We seek the fight
With falchions bright,
With our hearts in brave communion—
Together we'll stand
For our glorious land,
And the cause of the grand old Union!

Oh! who would shrink
From danger's brink,
Or fly from the conflict gory,
When Ruin complete
Will attend defeat,
While Victory crowns with glory!
We'll dare the fight
For Freedom's right,
With hearts in brave communion!
Together we'll stand
For our glorious land,
And the cause of the grand old Union!

Remember Traitors.

AIR—*Boyne Water.*

When Union ruled our noble land,
    And Liberty's arms were round her,
No foemen could her power withstand,
    No danger could astound her.
But now, in rebel ranks displayed,
    With despot snares behind them,
Old friends we see as foes arrayed,
    And mark them, as we find them!

We mark the wretch, where'er he be,
    Who's false to the land that bore him;
We'll mark the knave who swears he's free,
    Yet brooks a traitor o'er him!
And more than all, we'll mark the men
    Whose traitorous inclination
Would rivet foreign chains again
    O'er Freedom's chosen nation!

When strangers sought Columbia's shore,
    And the wanderer claimed protection,
We bade them share our peaceful store,
    And asked no mean subjection.
And now, thank God! when Treason's band
    Conspire in vile communion,
We see the sons of every land
    Combined to shield our Union!

Beautiful Union.

AIR—*Beautiful Venice.*

Beautiful Union! Liberty's home!
More queenly than Greece, more immortal than
    Rome!
How fondly thy name in our love is enshrined—
How close to all hearts are thy glories entwined;
For Freedom's bright banner waves over thy soil,
And beneath it, secure, every freeman may toil;
For of all the world's lands there is no land like
    thee,
My Beautiful Union! The Land of the Free!

Beautiful Union! Pride of the earth!
With thee all the hopes of the people had birth;
Thy shores are their refuge from tyranny's ban—
Where justice and freedom are pledged unto man!
And the dastard who doubts thee, the wretch who
    betrays,
Accursed of all mankind shall end his vile days!
For of all the world's lands, there is no land like
    thee—
Our Beautiful Union! the Land of the Free!

The Star-Gemmed Flag.

Our fathers cleft the ocean wave,
The birthright of the free to save;
And when they hail'd these western shores,
They claim'd them as their own and ours.
And when a Prince of foreign lands
His warriors poured upon our strands,
They spurned the lordlings from their fields,
And o'er their homes still held their shields.
Then wave the Flag, our Fathers' Flag,
   In memories of their bravery;
Then shout the Flag, our Fathers' Flag,
  The Star-gemmed Flag of brave hearts and the free.

CHORUS.

Run up the Flag, unfold the Flag,
   Broad as the land, wide as the sea;
Then wave the Flag, then cheer the Flag,
   The star-gemmed Flag of brave hearts and the free.

Our mothers by our fathers stood,
As if, in war, they had been wooed;
Tho' fragile were their yielding forms
While rolled the war-cloud and the storms.
And yet, heroic as their lords,
They cheered with smiles, with tears, with words.
But while they trembled at their homes,
They leaned on God whence victory comes.
Then shout the Flag, our Mothers' Flag,
   In memory of their well-spent lives;
Then wave the Flag, our Mothers' Flag,
  The Star-gemmed Flag of brave hearts and their
      wives.

Our Sisters, too, were bravely dear,
They gave their smiles, they wept their tear;
And rested in their mothers' arms,
Or often woke to war's alarms.
But while their hearts in sorrows moved,
And wept the brothers that they loved,
They knew the strife was for the free,
Their Country and for Liberty.
Then hail the Flag, our Sisters' Flag,
   Its Stars and Stripes their zones shall be;
Then wave the Flag, our Sisters' Flag,
   The Star-gemmed Flag our Sisters' zones shall be.

A seven-years' war was past and gone,
And many a heart was left forlorn;
But prouder o'er our Western shore,
Its Eagle-Bird was seen to soar;
And in his talons, as he flies,
He bears our Flag of victories;
And ever shall that Banner be,
The hope, the shield of Liberty.
Then shout the Flag, our Country's Flag,
   The Banner-Flag of Liberty;
Then wave the Flag, our UNION'S Flag,
   The Star-gemmed Flag of brave hearts and the free.

And on the land, and on the sea,
Wherever roam her sons from thee,
Our Nation's Flag shall ope its fold,
The loved and honored of the world;
For right, not might shall be its claim,
As "Flag of Freedom" is its name;
While Armies shall our emblem bear,
And Navies our proud bunting wear.
Then shout the Flag, our Army's flag,
   The Flag of Right and Liberty;
Then hail the Flag, our Navy's Flag,
   The Star-gemmed Flag of brave hearts and the free.

Words of Sympathy.

BY ROBERT M. HART.

AIR—Katy Darling.

Oh, they told us you were dead, poor Jeff. Davis,
    That your form was lying stiff and cold
In the catacombs of Eastern Virginia,
    Where thy virtues were greatly extolled ;
But, oh, 'twas a cruel hoax, Jeff. Davis,
    You're alive and kicking, we see,
And there's many now would hang you, poor Jeff.
        Davis,
    On the branch of the first sycamore tree.

Your pockets they are empty, poor Jeff. Davis,
    And of gold you are very much in need,
While starvation mounts the throne close beside you,
    And secession has just gone to seed ;
And, oh, what a sad mistake, Jeff. Davis,
    To think with cotton all alone
You could frighten Uncle Sam, poor Jeff. Davis,
    And then rob him of half of his home.

Oh, there's trouble in the South, poor Jeff. Davis,
    And your prestige is going to decay ;
You had better get your duds ready shortly,
    And push forward, an exile, this way,
We'll *feed* you and *lodge* you, Jeff. Davis—
    Our kindness you ne'er will forget—
We'll take you out a sailing, poor Jeff. Davis,
    And then land you at Fort Lafayette.

Volunteer's Song.

AIR—*Free and Easy.*

Onward! onward! is the cry now,
　Treason stalks throughout the land;
To guard our honor each one try now,
　March together, heart and hand.

CHORUS.

So let the Southerners do as they will,
We will fight for the Union still!
　　Fight for the Union!
　　Fight for the Union!
We will fight for the Union still!

Though Revolution, dark as night,
　Enshrouds the Banner of the Free,
There are none so base that will not fight
　For this great land of Liberty!

The traitors would the Union sever
　Our fathers worked so hard to form;
Yet we are for the Union ever,
　Through sunshine, peace, or storm!

Then hear! Oh hear! our country's call,
　Raise our glorious banner high;
Come, rally! rally! one and all!
　To save the Union or to die!

A Mother's Hymn in Time of War.

BY WILLIAM ROSS WALLACE.

Oh Lord of hosts! his country called,
    And nobly to her voice he sprung,
While o'er his brow our banner flashed,
    Where chargers neighed and trumpets rung.
There were no tremors in his eye,
    When putting on his warrior-crest;
And but a tear—it was when he
    Was clasped unto his mother's breast!

Oh Father! shield him from the shot;
    But if it is his doom to die,
May he, with shouts of triumph round,
    Bend on our flag his closing eye—
And feeling that his mother's soul
    Is watching on the field of death;
Where, though it weeps, yet gives a smile]
    Unto her brave boy's last wild breath.

Oh, proudly will his mother see
    Her Country wreathe his hero-tomb,
And many a Spring nurse tenderly,
    With nature's tears, the garland's bloom!
How sweet will be the song of praise,
    Where his dear relics peaceful lie!
How grand—away exultant thoughts!
    Oh God! he must not, *must not* die!

Away to the Fray.

AIR—*The Sea—the Sea.*

Oh, away! away! to the mighty fray,
  To the strife for all most dear ;
There is naught on earth of a rarer worth,
  Than a patriot's faith sincere !
And the cause that calls us all this day,
  Is the holiest cause that e'er
Invoked the aid of a brave man's blade,
  Or the power of a good man's prayer.

CHORUS.

Away ! away ! let cowards stay !
  But honor impels the brave !
There's naught but death in a craven's years,
  And there's life in a hero's grave.

When the cause we serve is a righteous cause,
  And the flag we bear unstained,
And our patriot steel, for the common weal,
  We lift, with hands unchained,
There is never a power can bar our path,
  Nor force can bid us turn,
Till we clasp our brands, with a victor's hands,
  Or they lie on the funeral urn !
      Away ! away ! etc.

The Union Gunning Match.

BY ROBERT M. HART.

AIR—*Johnny Stole the Ham.*

The Union boys are all out gunning,
   Are all out gunning, are all out gunning—
The Union boys are all out gunning—
   Oh listen to the noise.

Chorus—Around the monster Tree
      That sprung from Liberty,
    'Twas nurtured by the Free
     And Union-loving boys.

Some *game* they caught and caged already,
   And caged already, and caged already—
Some game they caught and caged already,
   Way down in Lafayette.

Chorus—There we can see the *birds*
     Who traveled North in herds,
    Because of deeds and words
     That Samuel can't forget.

Our Sam's awake, and both eyes open,
   And both eyes open, and both eyes open,
Our Sam's awake, and both eyes open,
   As umpire of the day.

Chorus—With good and steady aim,
     And ardor none can tame,
    Our boys the match will gain—
     The laurel bear away.

The stakes are up, the ground all ready,
   The ground all ready, the ground all ready—
The stakes are up, the ground all ready,
   And now, boys, blaze away.

Chorus—But hark the sudden news!
     Old Jeff. has got the blues,
    And trembling in his shoes—
     Secesh has gone astray.

The Nation of the Free.

BY MRS. METTA V. VICTOR.

Oh, mother of a matchless race !
  Columbia, hear our cry;
The children nursed in your embrace,
  For you will live and die.
We glory in our fathers' deeds,
  We love the soil they trod;
Our heritage we will defend
  And keep, so help us God !

CHORUS.

Rise, rise ! Oh Patriots, rise !
  Let waiting millions see !
What courage thrills, what faith inspires
  The Nation of the Free !

Hail, brothers in a common cause !
  True to your birthright stand !
The Constitution and the Laws
  Must know no Vandal hand.
Let foreign foes invidious gaze,
  To see our light expire ;
They'll shrink in awe before the blaze
  Of Freedom's deathless fire.

Hark ! how the hymns of glory swell
  Above our fathers' graves !
Th' unfaltering men of Seventy-Six
  Begot no race of slaves.
The blood that bought our sacred right
  Still in their lineage runs ;
No tribute gold, no traitor's might
  Shall wrest it from their sons.

Shade of heroic Washington !
  Still guard our Native Land !
Rebuke, rebuke each wavering one,
  Direct each ardent hand !
Oh, mother of a matchless race !
  Hear our united cry !
'Tis noble in your cause to live,
  And nobler still to die !

The Stars and Stripes.

Rally round the flag, boys—
Give it to the breeze!
That's the banner *we* love,
On the land and seas.

Brave hearts are under it;
Let the *Traitors* brag;
Gallant lads, fire away!
And fight for the flag.

Their flag is but a rag—
Ours is the *true* one;
Up with the Stars and Stripes!
Down with the new one!

Let our colors fly, boys—
Guard them day and night;
For Victory is Liberty,
And God will bless the Right.

The "Mud-Sills" Greeting.

Air—*Yankee Doodle.*

Oh nigger-drivers, don't you know
    You ought to have a thrashing,
For kicking up this mighty row—
    This game of Union-smashing?
Not satisfied with what you've got,
    You want to bag and steal, sirs,
Our Capitol and capital—
    With Jonathan you've to deal, sirs!

CHORUS.

So corn-cobs twist your hair,
    Gun-wheels run around you,
Alligators drag you off,
    And empty kegs surround you!

The "mud-sills" have at length got tired
    Of insolence and treason;
They'll teach the rebels an all-fired
    Lesson for the season.
Then sneak behind masked batteries,
    Lay down in your trenches,
Send the darkies out on guard,
    Make armorers of their wenches,

CHORUS.

Yankee boys will make you hear
    Constitution's thunder!
Yankee blades in Yankee hands
    Will fill your souls with wonder.

The Past and Present.

BY ROBERT M. HART.

AIR—*Old Bob Ridley O.*

Old Abram came across the mountains,
By rural cots and gushing fountains,
To rule a great and happy nation—
And the brightest gem in all creation;
    Old Abe Lincoln O, old Abe Lincoln O,
    Our hearts are true to stand by you,
        Abram Lincoln O.

When Abe took charge of our plantation,
Secesh was making preparation
To steal the half for raising cotton,
But soon found out his scheme was rotten;
    Old Abe Lincoln O, Old Abe Lincoln O,
    No mercy show the thieving foe,
        Abram Lincoln O.

Old Abram is a man of knowledge,
Although he never went to college,
And his heart is right, and strong his nerve,
And from his duty will not swerve;
    Old Abe Lincoln O, old Abe Lincoln O,
    Hold up the Flag and never lag,
        Abram Lincoln O.

Old Abe goes in for home protection,
And keeps an army of inspection,
Just to see that things are done up right,
And the boys are spoiling for a fight;
    Old Abe Lincoln O, old Abe Lincoln O,
    When they begin, let them go in,
        Abram Lincoln O.

Song of Union.

Air—*Zuyder Zee.*

Grand is the sight, when for national right,
    A People in arms are rising—
Every bosom on fire with a freeman's desire,
    Every spirit all treason despising.
Crying—" Oh, let the Song of Union be
Strong and deep as the rolling sea !
Deep and strong as the rolling sea !"

Grand is the cause of our Land and Laws,
    And the good old Constitution !
For our lives and gold, and our honor, we hold
    Like the men of the Revolution !
Crying—" Oh, let the Song of Union be
Strong and deep as the rolling sea !
Deep and strong as the rolling sea !"

Rise, brothers, rise !—let your mingling cries,
    Roll out in a grand hosanna !
March, brothers, march ! while the stars o'erarch,
    We have always our country's banner !
Crying—" Oh, let the Song of Union be
Strong and deep as the rolling sea !
Deep and strong as the rolling sea !"

Traitor, Spare that Flag.

BY THOMAS MACEVILY.

AIR—*Woodman, Spare that Tree.*

Traitors, spare that flag!
  Look up at its bright folds,
And see within your hearts,
  The baseness of your souls;
For that's the proud old flag
  Your sires oft fought under—
Are you, degenerate sons,
  To tear it now asunder?

Traitors, spare that flag!
  Or vengeance loud and deep
Will justly fall from Heaven,
  And make you one day weep;
And the ashes of your fathers
  Will rise from out the tomb
'Gainst their ungrateful dastards,
  To curse the traitor's doom.

Traitors, spare that flag!
  If you would yet be free—
If you've the least regard
  For homes and liberty;
If not, why, do your best;
  We've men and means at hand
To spread it to the breeze
  O'er all Columbia's land.

Traitors, spare that flag!
  You've done mischief enough:
You've stolen our gold and guns,
  And talked vain boasting stuff;
Then, touch not that proud flag,
  That banner of the free,
Lest vengeance dire and deep
  May engulf you in misery.

A Life in the Soldier's Camp.

BY JAS. O'C., COMPANY D, ANDERSON ZOUAVES.

Air—*Life on the Ocean Wave.*

A life in the soldier's camp,
  A home in the snow-white tent,
Where we hear the sentry tramp,
  And merry hours are spent;
Where glory waits the brave,
  On the bloody battle-field,
And the Stars and Stripes shall wave,
  O'er Zouaves that never yield.

Come, shoulder your musket, boys,
  And off to the field of strife;
Leave home, and all its joys,
  And fly to a soldier's life—
With knapsack on your back,
  And canteen by your side—
To follow the foeman's track,
  Is the brave young Zouave's pride.

The camp is the place for me,
  When my country calls me there,
To fight for the Flag of the Free,
  I'd live on homeliest fare;
When the tattoo beats at night,
  And the reveille in the morn,
And the Zouave's heart is light
  As soon as the day is born.

Then farewell, home and friends,
  For I've joined the volunteers;
I'll be with him who defends
  Our Flag, and never fears.
I'm off for the Zouaves' camp,
  I'm bound for Freedom's Wars;
On the rebel flag I'll tramp,
  And fight for the Stripes and Stars.

A Soldier's Dream of Home,

BY WILLIAM ADAMS.

Inscribed to Lieut. A. C. CALKINS, 21st (Buffalo) Reg't, N. Y. S. V.

AIR—*America.*

Still is the mighty host,
Each sentry at his post,
  'Tis midnight's hour:
There on my pallet low,
My brain on fire—aglow
With scenes of long-ago—
  Entrancing power!

Home of my boyhood's hours,
Nestled 'mid shady bowers,
  How dear thou art!
I'm with you once again,
Freed from the poignant pain
Of seeing brothers slain—
  Never to part.

Kind friends and parents dear,
Brushing the silent tear,
  Utter, "Welcome!
Let glee and joy abound,
Let songs and jokes go round,
A warrior's here—we've found
  Our only son!"

A ramble now I take
O'er glen and silvery lake,
  Now doubly dear!
Slowly I tread South Hill,
Thro' wood and over rill,
The buzz of yon old mill
  Reaching my ear.

Alas! how brief the stay!
A twinkling—then away
  From scenes I love!
Back to the battle-field,
Where wounded patriots bleed,
From harm, be Thou my shield,
  Oh God! above.

A Yankee Volunteer.

I thought I'd better come to town,
  I brought along my gun, sir;
We guessed quite likely there'd be work,
  Or praps there might be fun, sir;
I heerd wild geese was plenty, now,
  A comin' from the south'ard,
And thought I'd like a shot at some—
  If you ain't too much bothered.

My father sends his duty, sir;
  He says that things is growin,'
And wants to know what he can do
  T' help the men that's goin'.
Mother, she looks kind o' scared,
  But fixed my things to come, sir;
She didn't want me, jest, to start,
  Nor jest to stay at home, sir.

There's brother Jim, he's fierce to fight,
  "Too young, boy," says the jury;
(Jim's seventeen) so he gets mad
  And works away like fury.
He's nigh about as tall as I,
  That's six foot and a quarter,
(Han't measured lately, but I guess
  I can't ha' grown much shorter.)

Now, what d'ye spose Jerusha said,
  With her black eyes a snappin'?
She's jest my second cousin, sir,
  One seldom caught a nappin'.
She said if she could see a man
  A fightin' for the flag, sir,
That she would give her new silk gown
  And call it but a rag, sir.

I'd meant before to come, for sure,
  But that was jest a clincher;
I never was a soldier, yit,
  But might be at a pinch, sir.
I'll try—and if my lamp goes out
  Afore their shot and brag, sir,
Jest tell Jerusha how I died
  A fightin' for the flag, sir.

Three Cheers for Our Banner.

Three cheers for our Banner, the Stripes and the Stars,
The ensign of Liberty's glorious wars!
Fling it out to the breezes, its colors display,
Let our Standard float boldly in face of the day.
We will stand by this Banner, through fire and flood,
We will guard and defend it, though crimson'd with
blood.

CHORUS.

Then three cheers for our Banner, in peace and in wars,
We will ever be true to the Stripes and the Stars.

Three cheers for our Union, the land of our birth;
'Tis the fortress of freedom, the hope of the earth;
Arouse you, ye sons of the East and the West,
To defend it, though blood flow from each gallant
breast;
Remember, a noble old poet has said,
'Tis sweet, for our country, to sleep with the dead.

The noble young heroes, who rescue her name,
Columbia will crown, with the garland of fame;
If they fall, she will weep o'er their glorious scars,
And will lay them to rest 'neath her Banner of Stars;
We know the Volunteers will always be found
In the van of the host, on the blood-redden'd ground.

Three cheers for Columbia, the queen of the world,
To the wind's every quarter her flag be unfurled;
We have bowed at her feet, in the day of her pride,
Shall we basely desert her, now she is defied?
No! millions of voices will instant reply,
For freedom and country, we'll dare and we'll die.

The Flag of the Brave.

Air—*Red, White and Blue.*

Our tars are the lords of the ocean,
    Our champions on the blue brine,
And 'mid the fierce battle's commotion
    Our banner, triumphant, shall shine !
They'll win a proud mention in story
    When cannon loud boom o'er the wave ;
They'll garland their banner with glory
    In fight, 'neath the Flag of the Brave !

CHORUS.

In fight 'neath the Flag of the Brave !
In fight 'neath the Flag of the Brave !
    They'll garland their banner with glory,
In fight 'neath the Flag of the Brave !

As long as a sail dots the ocean,
    Or sea-breezes blow o'er the deep,
As long as the earth keeps in motion,
    Or stars their lone vigils shall keep—
So long shall Columbia's brave seamen
    Be monarchs upon the salt wave :
Three cheers for the valor of Freemen !
    Three cheers for the Flag of the Brave !
Chorus—Three cheers for the Flag of the Brave !
    Three cheers for the Flag of the Brave !
      Three cheers for the valor of freemen !
    Three cheers for the Flag of the Brave !

The Patriot Soldier.

Air—*America, Commerce and Freedom.*

How proud the steps a soldier treads,
　His country's cause defending;
And dear the blood a freeman sheds,
　With glory's laurels blending;
Though fiery tempest sweep his path,
　In battle's line appearing,
And death draw nigh, in lurid wrath,
　All horrid shapes uprearing,

CHORUS.

Still, gallant and brave, he smiles at the grave,
　And hastes to his comrades, to lead them;
In the field of red Mars, 'neath the Banner of Stars,
　His war-cry is "Union and Freedom!"

In all the land, from South to North,
　From East to West, he glories;
But fights to drive the traitors forth,
　And rid its soil of tories!
No crafty words his faith can shake—
　No force can make him falter;
He draws his sword for Union's sake,
　And strikes for Freedom's altar!
For, gallant and brave, he smiles at the grave,
　And flies to his comrades, to lead them;
In the field of red Mars, 'neath the Banner of Stars,
　His war-cry is "Union and Freedom!"

Give us Room.

Air—*Buy a Broom.*

From Northland we come with our sharp-shooting
rifles,
To chase Southern traitors from Liberty's soil ;
All heedless of Bull-Runs or such passing trifles,
We're bound to march onward, through danger
or toil.

CHORUS.

Give us room ! give us room !
Give us room ! give us room !
Our sharp-shooting rifles shall make for us room.

From Sumter we first heard the cannon's loud boom-
ing—
O'er crimson Potomac the sound rose again ;
And now from Missouri, where war-clouds are loom-
ing,
We hear the loud summons of true-hearted men.
Give us room ! give us room !
Give us room ! give us room !
Our sharp-shooting rifles will soon make us room.

Brave Cameron lies low with the sods of the valley,
And Lyon's bold bosom is cold in the grave ;
But again for the conflict their comrades still rally,
And pour out for Union the blood of the brave.
Give us room ! give us room !
Give us room ! give us room !
Our sharp-shooting rifles shall soon make us room.

The Union Marseillaise.

AIR— *The Marseilles Hymn.*

Arise! Arise! ye sons, of patriot sires!
    A Nation calls! and Heaven speed your **way.**
Now Freedom lights anew her waning fires,
    And spreads her banner to the day,
    And spreads her banner to the day.
While to His Throne our hearts are swelling,
    Freedom, and Law, and Truth, and Right,
    May God defend by his own might,
By his right arm the treason quelling
        Ye loyal sons, and true,
           Sons of the brave and free,
      Join hearts, join hands, to strike **anew**
        For God and Liberty.

With faith your all to Him confiding
    Who crowned with victory our fathers' **hand,**
With courage in his strength abiding,
    Go forth in Freedom's sacred band,
    Go forth to save our native land.
Defend from faction's wild commotion,
    Our homes, our laws, our schools and **spires,**
    The names and graves of patriot sires,
Till Freedom reigns to furthest ocean.
        Ye loyal sons and true,
          Sons of the brave and free,
      Join hearts, join hands, to strike **anew**
        For God and Liberty.

The Alarum.

BY R. H. STODDARD.

Men of the North and West,
  Wake in your might,
Prepare, as the Rebels have done,
  For the fight;
You cannot shrink from the test,
Rise! Men of the North and West!

They have torn down your banner of stars;
  They have trampled the laws;
They have stifled the freedom they hate,
  For no cause!
Do you love it, or slavery best?
Speak! Men of the North and West.

They strike at the life of the State—
  Shall the murder be done?
They cry, " We are two!" And you?
  " *We are one!*"
You must meet them, then, breast to breast,
On! men of the North and West!

Not with words—they laugh them to scorn,
  And tears they despise;
But with swords in your hands, and death
  In your eyes!
Strike home! leave to God all the rest,
Strike! Men of the North and West!

Battle Invocation.

BY JAMES G. CLARK.

Air—The Assyrian came down, etc.

Oh! spirits of Washington, Warren and Wayne!
Oh! shades of the Heroes and Patriots slain!
Come down from your mountains of emerald and gold,
And smile on the Banner ye cherished of old.

Descend in your glorified ranks to the strife,
Like legions sent forth from the armies of life;
Let us feel your deep presence, as waves feel the breeze
When the white fleets, like snow-flakes, are drank by
    the seas.

Proud sons of the soil where the Palmetto grows,
Once patriots and brothers, now traitors and foes,
Ye have turned from the path which our forefathers'
    trod,
And stolen from man the best gift of his God.

Ye have trampled the tendrils of love in the ground,
Ye have scoffed at the law which the Nazarene found,
Till the great wheel of Justice seemed blocked for a
    time,
And the eyes of humanity blinded with crime.

As the vail which conceals the clear starlight is riven
When clouds strike together, by warring winds driven,
So the blood of the race must be offered like rain,
Ere the stars of our country are ransomed again.

The Patriot's Address.

AIR—*Scots Wha Hae.*

Patriot hearts and loyal souls !
Ye whose faith no fear controls—
Lo ! the storm of treason rolls
    Round your glorious liberty !
Rebel swords have struck your shield—
Traitor hands their poniards wield—
Miscreant tyrants bid ye yield
    Power and place to slavery !

By your ancient heroes' blood,
By their deeds on field and flood ;
By the fruits of Freedom's bud,
    Sprung from northern loyalty—
Strike at once these daring foes—
Round their soil your legions close—
Bid them drain the cup of woes.
    They would fill for you and me.

Heaven is on the Freeman's side—
God still rules the battle's tide—
Heaven and God *they* have defied,
    Who make war for slavery !
Let them feel a patriot's ire,
Withering all their base desire—
Let our anger be as fire,
    Blasting chains and tyranny !

The Patriot's Wish.

BY ROBERT M. HART.

Air—*The Star-Spangled Banner.*

Oh God bless our land, and united once more,
  May we gather true wisdom from war's desolation;
From the thick curling smoke, and the fierce cannon's roar,
  Let peace in her beauty rise and smile on our nation;
To show to the world that peace is unfurled,
And war from Columbia forever is hurled.

CHORUS.

That the proud Ark of Freedom, with bold, trusty crew,
Still sails 'neath the banner of the Red, White and Blue.

Great God bless our land, for 'tis dyed in the gore
  Of the good and the brave of a nation's defenders;
Oh! may death's fearful havoc molest us no more,
  And Thy love fill the bosom as passion surrenders;
To show to the world that love is unfurled,
And hate from Columbia forever is hurled.
        That the proud Ark, etc.

Oh God bless our land—may our eagle still fly,
  And gaze on Columbia in proud adoration;
Let the sunlight of truth ever flash from his eye,
  Urging freemen to duty in dark tribulation;
To show to the world that truth is unfurled,
Aught else from Columbia forever is hurled.
        That the proud Ark, etc.

May the emblem we love, the Flag of the Free,
  For all time to come be our shield and our protection,
Ever waving in glory on land and on sea,
  Our shrine of devotion and fond recollection;
To show to the world our flag is unfurled,
And strife from Columbia forever is hurled.
        That the proud Ark, etc.

The Union Harvesting.

AIR—*Old Oaken Bucket.*

Oh, fair is the orchard, with russet fruit laden,
   And bright is the cornfield, all golden with grain,
And sweet is the garden, where matron and maiden,
   Sit listening at eve to the whippowil's strain;
But fairer, and brighter, and sweeter, and dearer,
   Are the orchards of crimson, the fields of bright red,
And the flow'rets immortal that hallow the wearer,
   Whose blood for his country is loyally shed,
In the orchards of Union, the cornfields of Union,
   The gardens of Union, for Liberty shed.

Though the reaper be Death, and his garner the charnel,
   And the wine-press o'erflow with our patriot blood—
Though the furrows run red with a vintage incarnal,
   Who will shrink from the field? who will pause
     at the flood?
Who will measure the grain while 'tis standing or
   falling?
Who will count what is lost, till the day shall be
   won?
While the sun shines aloft, while the Master is calling,
   In the field be our place, till the field-work is done!
In the orchards of Union, the cornfields of Union,
   The gardens of Union, till victory is won.

Beadle's Dime Song Books.

No. 1.

All's for the best.
A good time coming
A national song,
A thousand a year,
Annie Laurie, [year,
Ans'er to thousand a
Ans'er to K.Kearney
Belle Brandon,
Ben Bolt,
Blind boy's lament,
Bob Ridley,
Bold private'r [home
Do they miss me at
Don't be angry,
Down the river,
Dying Californian,
E Pluribus Unum,
Evening star,
Faded flowers,
Gentle Annie,
Gentle Jennie Gray,
Glad to get home,
Hard times, [sister,
Have you seen my
Heather dale,
Hills of NewEngland
Home again,
I am not angry,
I want to go home,
Juney at the gate,
Kate Kearney,
Kiss me quick and go
Kitty Clyde,
Little Blacksmith,
Marseilles hymn,
Miller of the Dee,
My home in Kentu'k
My own native land,
Nelly Gray,
Nelly was a lady,
Old dog Tray,
Old folks we loved.
Our Mary Ann,
Over the mount_in,
Poor old slave,
Red, white and blue,
Root, hog, or die--1,
Row, row, [2, 3 & 4.
Shells of the ocean,
Song of the sexton,
Sword of Bunk'r hill
Star spangled ban'er

The age of progress,
The lake-side shore,
The old farm-house,
The old play-ground
The rock of liberty,
The tempest,
Twenty years ago,
Twinkling stars,
Uncle Sam's farm,
Unfurl the banner,
Wait for the wagon,
Willie, we've missed
Willie,roam no more

No. 2

Alice Gray,
America,
Banks of Mohawk,
Be kind to each oth'r
Billy Grimes, rover,
Bryan O'Lynn,
Come, sit thee down
Cora Lee,
Crazy Jane,
Darling Nelly Moore
Darling old stick,
Fireman's victory,
Good news from
Good-night, [home,
Grave of Lilly Dale,
Graves of household
Home, sweet home,
I've no mother now,
I'm going home,
I'm leaving thee in
I miss thee, [sorrow,
Irishman's shanty,
I wandered by the
Katy Darling,[brook
Kathl'n Movourneen
Little Katy,
Mary of wild moor,
_abel Clare,
Mary Aileen,
Mill May,
Minnie Moore,
Minnie dear,
Mrs. Lofty and I,
Mr. Finagan,
My eye and B.Martin
My love is a sailer,
My mother dear,
My grandma's advice

My mother's bible,
Nancy Bell,
New England,
Oh! the sea, the sea,
Old folks are gone,
Old sideling hill,
Our boyhood days,
Our fatherland,
Peter Gray,
Rory O'Moore,
Scorn not thy broth'r
Shouldn't like to tell
Somebody's waiting
The farmer sat,
The farmer's boy,
The postboy's song,
The quilting party,
Three bells, [heart is
'Tis home where the
Waiting for the May
We stand united,
Where bright waves
What other name,
What's home with-
Winter, [out mother
Widow Machree,
Willie's on the sea.

No. 3.

Annie, dear, good-by
A sailor's life for me
Answer to Jeannette
Bessie was a bride,
Bonnie Jean,
Boys of Kilkenny,
Comic Katy Darling
Comic parody,
Darling Jennie Bell,
Darling Rosabel,
Death of An'e Laurie
Emigrant's farewell,
Ettie May,
Few days,
Fine old Eng. Gent.,
Fine old Irish Gent.,
Fine old Dutchman,
Fireman's death,
Girl in a calico dress
Give 'em string,
Girl I left behind me
Golddigger's lament
Go it while young,
Hail Columbia,

(2)

Roll on, silver moon
Sambo, I've missed,
Sammy Slap,
Simon, the cellarer,
Someth'g to love me
Some love to drink,
Sourkrout and sau's
The gay cavalier,
The gambler's wife,
The ingle side,
The ivy green,
The monks of old,
The musical wife,
The ocean burial,
The old arm-chair,
The watcher,
Tail iv me coat,
Thou art gone,
Thou hast wounded,
'Tis midnight hour,
Twilight dews,
Umbrella courtship,
Wake, Dinah, wake,
Washington,
We'll have a dance,
We met by chance,
When I saw Nelly,
When the swallows
Whoop de doodle do
William of the ferry,
Will you love me.

No. 6.

Annie Lisle,
Beautiful world,
Be kind to the loved
Bloom is on the rye,
Bobbin' around,
Bonnie Dundee,
Cottage of mother,
Courting in Coun't,
Dearest Mae,
Dear mother, I come
Ella Ree,
Fairy Dell,
Far, far upon the sea
Female auctioneer,
Gentle Hallie,
Gentle Nettie Moore
Happy we to-night,
Hattie Lee,
He doeth all things,
Home without sister
I can't call her mot'r

I'll paddle my canoe,
I'm stand'g by grave
Irish jaunting car,
Is it anybody's bus's
Jane O'Mally,
Jenny Lane,
Joanna Snow,
Johnny Sands,
Lilly Dale,
Little more cider,
Lords of creation,
Lulu is our pride,
Marion Lee,
Meet me by the br'k
Merry sleighride,
Minnie Clyde,
Mountaineer's fare'l
Not for gold,
Not married yet,
Oh, carry me home,
Old homestead,
Old mountain tree,
Ossian's serenade,
Over the river,
Riding on a rail,
Sailor boy's dream,
Say yes, pussy,
Silber shining moon
Song my mot'r sang,
Spare the homestead
Spirit-voice of Belle,
Squire Jone's dau'r,
The blue Junietta,
The carrier-dove,
The child's wish,
The maniac,
The May-queen,
The miller's maid,
The modern belle,
The strawberry girl,
The snow-storm,
Three grains of corn
Washington's grave,
Where are friends,
Why chime the bells
Why don't the men,
Will nobody marry,
Young recruit.

No 7

A ride I was taking,
Anchor's weighed,
Beautiful Venice,
Billy Patterson,

Breeze of the night,
Bright-eyed Nell,
Come, Willie dear,
Deal with me kindly
Dixie's Land, 1 & 2,
Doley Jones,
Don't you remember
Down in cane-brakes
Fairy Belle,
Farewell, cottage,
Glendy burk,
Ho, Gondolier, wake
How shall I watch,
Hush-a-by, baby,
I love my nat. land,
I'm a jolly bachelor,
It is recorded,
Julianna Johnson,
Lilly Ray,
Little Daisy,
Little Ella,
Maggie by my side,
Maggie, pride of vale
Mary May,
Mary's welcome,
Massa in cold gro'nd
Massa sound sleep'g
My brodder Gum,
My canoe's on Ohio,
My old house,
My mountain home,
Nelly Bly,
Newfoundland dog,
No, thank you, sir,
Old ironsides,
Old K. Y. Ky,
Our Union,'r't or w'g
Over the summer sea
Paddy Boohree,
Queen Mary's escape
Revolutionary times
Ring de banjo,
Roy Neill,
She's black,
Some folks,
Star of my home.
Take me home to die
The evening gun,
The happy Switzer,
The home I leave,
The messenger bird,
The old stage-coach,
The pilot,
The reefer's song,
The ship on fire,

(3)

The sleighing glee,
Under the willow,
Virginia Belle,
Way down in Cairo,
We're coming, sister
Who'll have me,
Willie, my brave.

No. 8.

A life on the ocean,
Annie of the vale,
A wet sheet,
Bonnie Eloise,
Brightly o'er lake
By the lone riverside
Campbells are com'g
Come by sil'ry brook
Come, maiden,
Down by the river,
Ella Leene,
Ellen Bayne,
Farewell, Lilly dear,
Farewell, mother,
Girls aren't so green
Going home to Dixie
Good-by, Linda love,
Happy be thy dreams
Hard times,
Home and friends,
Home I leave behind
I'd be a Gipsey,
I'd rather be a violet
If I had one to love,
I had a dream,
I'm o'er young,
I'm queen of village,
I'm thinking of thee
I see her in dreams,
Jeanie with the
Jennie's coming o'er
Katie's secret,
Kinlock of Kinlock,
Kitty dear,
Kitty Wells,
Light of other days,
List to the mocking,
Little Jennie Dow,
Lizzie dies to-night,
Lone starry hours,
Long weary day,
Lost Rosabel,
Mary Avourneen,
Meeting of waters,
Near the banks of,

Old black Joe,
Old folks at home,
Riding in a ra'd keer
Rock me to sleep,
Row, row, brothers,
Row your boat,
Scenes brightest,
She wept her life,
Sighing for thee,
Silvery midn't moon
Some one to love,
Take me to Tennes'e
Tapping at window,
The brave old oak,
The dream is past,
The sea, the sea,
The wild rose,
The Zingarina,
'Tis but a faded flo'er
Vive L'America,
We'll meet in heaven
Western trap'rs song
What are wild waves
What fair'like music
Why have my loved,
Whistle and I come.

No. 9.

A maiden's prayer,
Basketmaker's child
Banks and braes,
Be quiet, do,
Bowld sojer boy,
Boys, carry me 'long
Bonnie new moon,
Bright moonlit sea,
Call me not unkind,
Canadian boat-song,
Castles in the air,
Come wh're moonb's
Come to de gum-tree
Come where my love
Cruiskeen Lawn,
Do they think of me
Do you remember,
Down at de barbecue
Eulalie,
Ever be happy,
Flow gently, Afton,
Female smuggler,
Gentle Bessie Gray,
Grave of Kitty Clyde
Hannah at the win'w
Harp of wild wind,

Hark, the vesper-h'n
Household clock,
I breathe my nat. air
I dream of mother,
I'll be no submissive
I'm not so ugly man,
Jamie's on the sea,
Jockey hat,
Joys we've tasted,
Johnny's so bashful,
Jennie's blue e'e,
Juanita,
Kind words,
Kissing through bars
Kiss me good-night,
Landlord's pet,
List to the convent,
Mary Blane,
Mine own,
Mother, I'm thinki'g
My mountain home,
My old Ky. home,
Nancy Till,
Negro Boatman song
Nettie is no more,
No one to love,
Not a star from flag,
Old schoolhouse,
Once more on sea,
Our laddie's dead,
Rouse, brothers,
Shall we know each
Sigh in the heart,
Silence and Tears,
Silver moonl't winds
Sleeping I dreamed,
Star of the twilight,
Teddy O'Neale,
That's what's matter
The blarney,
The captain,
The miller's song,
Three fishers,
'Way down in Maine
Widow Malone,
Woman's resolution

(4)

(5)

* 9 7 8 3 3 3 7 3 0 6 4 7 2 *